GRAPHIC BIOGRAPHIES
MARTIN LUTHER
KING JR.
THE LIFE OF A CIVIL RIGHTS LEADER

by
GARY JEFFREY
illustrated by
CHRIS FORSEY

Rosen Classroom Books & Materials ™
New York

Published in 2007 by The Rosen Publishing Group, Inc.
29 East 21st Street, New York, NY 10010

First edition, 2007

Designed and produced by
David West Books

Editor: Dominique Crowley
Photo Research: Victoria Cook

Photo credits:
page 4 Library of Congress; page 5 (top, middle, bottom) Library of Congress; page 6 (top, bottom) Library of Congress; page 7 (top, bottom) Library of Congress; page 44 SIPA/REX FEATURES; page 45 Library of Congress

Library of Congress Cataloging-in-Publication Data

Jeffrey, Gary.
Martin Luther King Jr.: the life of a civil rights leader / Gary Jeffrey; illustrated by Chris Forsey.—1st ed. p. cm–(Graphic biographies)
ISBN 10: 1-4042-0858-5 (library binding)
ISBN 13: 978-1-4042-0858-2 (library binding)
ISBN 10: 1-4042-0921-2 (pbk.)
ISBN 13: 978-1-4042-0921-3 (pbk.)
6-Pack ISBN 10: 1-4042-0920-4
6-Pack ISBN 13: 978-1-4042-0920-6
1. King, Martin Luther Jr., 1929–1968—Juvenile literature. 2. African Americans—Biography—Juvenile literature. 3. Civil rights workers—United States—Biography—Juvenile literature. 4. Baptists—United States—Clergy—Biography–Juvenile literature. 5. African Americans—Civil rights—History—20th century—Juvenile literature. I. Jeffrey, Gary, ill. II. Title. III. Series: Graphic biographies (Rosen Publishing Group)
E185.97.K5J43 2007
323.092—dc22

                                                                    2005035525

Manufactured in China

CONTENTS

WHO'S WHO

Martin Luther King Jr. (1929–1968) Born in Atlanta and the son of a preacher, King worked to improve the lives of minority groups, especially those of African Americans in the South.

Coretta Scott King (1927–2006) The wife of Martin Luther King Jr. and mother of their four children, Coretta studied music at Boston University, where she and King first met. She was also involved in civil rights work.

President John. F. Kennedy (1917–1963) Kennedy was the U.S. president who worked with King regarding African Americans' civil rights.

Ralph Abernathy (1926 –1990) Baptist Church pastor and close friend of Martin Luther King Jr., Abernathy was heavily involved in King's campaign to achieve equal rights for everyone.

Rosa Parks (1913–2005) Parks refused to give up her seat on a bus to a white person, as required by law. Her action caused the Montgomery Bus Boycott of 1955.

President Lyndon Baines Johnson (1907–1973) Johnson was the 36th president of the United States. He championed civil rights.

FREEDOM'S PROMISE

*A*t the end of the American Civil War in *1865, African Americans were no longer slaves but they still weren't free. How would they live successfully in a world that was hostile toward them?*

FREEDOM'S FATHER
In 1862, during the American Civil War, President Lincoln passed a law that freed slaves in the States.

FALSE FREEDOM

Changes to the American Constitution between 1866 and 1877 gave black people new rights. They were allowed to vote and to take an active part in the political process. They were also given the right to purchase the land of their former owners and to use all public buildings.

Before the Civil War, certain states had laws that prevented education of slaves. These states were known as "slave states" and included Louisiana and Alabama among others in the South. After the Civil War, former slaves crowded into newly built schools to learn to read and write. Racists, however, were quietly uniting against them, waiting to strike out openly.

They got their chance in 1883 when the Supreme Court ruled that the Civil Rights Act of 1875 was unconstitutional. Following this, Southern states passed laws that kept black people apart from white people. Then, in 1890, a law in Louisiana stated that black people must ride in separate railroad cars from whites. African Americans in Louisiana challenged the law. A local judge and, later, the U.S. Supreme Court, ruled against them. Acceptance of what came to be known as the Jim Crow laws had begun.

EARLY CAMPAIGNERS

The period from the 1890s to the start of World War I in 1914 was a difficult time for those fighting for racial equality. Liberty, won after the Civil War, was soon lost as African Americans were not always treated equally by white society. Racial violence was also at an all-time high. Yet, during these dark times, two strong leaders emerged.

BOOKER T. WASHINGTON

Booker T. Washington was born into slavery in Virginia and had achieved success through hard work. He believed that education was the way to create a proud and strong black society that could exist alongside a white one.

William Edward Burghardt Dubois was born in Massachusetts and was a university graduate. He was the first African American to be elected to the board of the National Association for the Advancement of Colored People (NAACP). This organization, founded in 1910 by both black and white people, believed in racial equality and fought for the civil rights of black Americans.

W. E. B. DUBOIS

THE JIM CROW LAWS

Named after a nineteenth-century stage character who mocked black people, the Jim Crow laws kept African Americans divided from white citizens. They promoted separate entrances and facilities in waiting rooms, movie theaters, restaurants, and even drinking fountains. Usually, the areas for African Americans were of a much lower standard than those for their white counterparts.

OUT OF SIGHT
A man uses the "colored" entrance to a Mississippi movie theater in 1939.

AMERICA DIVIDED

In 1941, President Franklin D. Roosevelt issued an executive order to allow the full participation of African Americans in the armed forces during World War II. This was at the request of a civil rights pressure group, and its victory made a big impression on the rest of African American society.

PROUD VETERANS
African Americans had fought and shed blood for four years alongside white people in World War II. Now they wanted equality at home.

RETURNING HOME

Southern African American veterans returning from World War II were often unwilling to suffer the humiliation of segregation, as they had before the war. Some whites, especially white supremacist groups like the Ku Klux Klan, felt that African Americans were an inferior race. As a result, acts of violence, including hangings in the South, were perpetrated against Blacks. This led to greater urgency among those fighting against racism, such as Martin Luther King Jr.

THE FIGHT FOR EQUAL RIGHTS

Working on a school segregation case in Charleston, South Carolina, NAACP lawyers convinced the Supreme Court to ban segregation in schools. The 1954 case marked a turning point in the fight for equal rights for African Americans. The decision desegregated Southern schools in 1957.

FIRST VICTORY
African Americans celebrate news of the 1954 Brown vs. Board of Education *case.*

THE BROTHERHOOD RISES

The first African American leader to use mass protest tactics against segregation laws was the labor leader A. Philip Randolph. In 1941, he threatened to lead a march on Washington, D.C., with hundreds of thousands of people to protest job discrimination in the military. The march never actually took place, but Randolph did eventually get his day. He was a co-organizer of one of the most famous marches for civil rights in American history, the March on Washington in 1963.

WHY SHOULD WE MARCH?

15.000 Negroes Assembled at St. Louis, Missouri
20.000 Negroes Assembled at Chicago, Illinois
23.500 Negroes Assembled at New York City
Millions of Negro Americans all Over This Great Land Claim the Right to be Free!

A CALL TO PROTEST
This flier was produced to encourage as many African Americans as possible to participate in the proposed march on Washington, D.C.

A PREACHER'S SON

Martin Luther King Jr. was born on January 15, 1929, in Atlanta, Georgia. At the time, Atlanta was heavily segregated. King would grow up to be one of the greatest preachers and speakers in history, taking after his father, Martin Luther King Sr., the pastor of a local church.

DR. MARTIN LUTHER KING JR.

GROWING UP IN ATLANTA, KING SAW SIGNS OF SEGREGATION EVERYWHERE IN THE CITY.

RESTROOMS, LUNCH COUNTERS, AND EVEN DRINKING FOUNTAINS WERE CLOSED TO PEOPLE OF HIS SKIN COLOR OR HAD SEPARATE ENTRANCES AND AREAS.

KING DID VERY WELL IN SCHOOL AND SHOWED AN EARLY TALENT FOR PUBLIC SPEAKING. DURING ELEVENTH GRADE, HE TOOK PART IN A SPEAKING CONTEST AT ANOTHER SCHOOL AND WAS TRAVELING HOME WITH A TEACHER WHEN...

MARTIN, YOU WON! YOUR PARENTS WILL BE SO PROUD!

IF I ACCEPT THAT IT'S THE SYSTEM THAT TURNS PEOPLE INTO RACISTS, THEN HOW DO I CHANGE THE SYSTEM?

AT CROZIER KING ATTENDED A LECTURE ABOUT THE INDIAN LEADER FOR PEACE, MAHATMA GHANDI.

GHANDI USED THE POWER OF LOVE AND TRUTH TO CREATE SOCIAL CHANGE.

LIKE GHANDI, I MUST CHANNEL MY ANGER INTO A POSITIVE AND CREATIVE FORCE!

HE READ ALL THE BOOKS HE COULD FIND ON GHANDI, PARTICULARLY ONE CALLED "THE POWER OF NONVIOLENCE."

REACTING TO HATRED WITH HATRED ONLY ADDS TO THE **BITTERNESS** OF THE WORLD. ONLY WHEN THE CHAIN OF HATRED IS CUT, CAN **BROTHERHOOD** BEGIN.

IN 1951, KING FINISHED AT THE TOP OF HIS CLASS AND WON A SCHOLARSHIP TO BOSTON UNIVERSITY, TO STUDY FOR A PH.D. IN APPLIED RELIGION. THERE, HE MET CORETTA SCOTT.

JANUARY 1954. DEXTER BAPTIST CHURCH, MONTGOMERY, ALABAMA.

THE CHURCH IS YOURS...IF YOU WANT IT, DR. KING.

I WILL BE SURE TO GIVE YOUR OFFER MY MOST PRAYERFUL CONSIDERATION!

ON THE FLIGHT HOME...

THIS IS NOT AN EASY CHOICE. THE STATE OF ALABAMA IS JUST ABOUT AS SEGREGATED AS THEY COME. IT WOULD NOT BE AN EASY LIFE FOR CORETTA AND ANY CHILDREN WE MAY HAVE.

BUT MAYBE IT'S WHERE I'M NEEDED MOST, IN THE BELLY OF THE BEAST. I COULD PREACH AGAINST SEGREGATION AND TAKE AN ACTIVE ROLE IN THE FIGHT.

ON APRIL 14, MARTIN LUTHER KING JR. BECAME PASTOR AT DEXTER BAPTIST CHURCH.

...GOMERY 1955. KING HAD BECOME ...S WITH FIRST BAPTIST CHURCH ...R RALPH ABERNATHY, AND E. B. NIXON, LEADER OF THE LOCAL STATE CHAPTERS OF THE NAACP.

IT IS AN ONGOING STRUGGLE. THE BIGGEST PROBLEM AT THE MOMENT IS WITH THE SEGREGATED CITY BUSES.

THE WHITE DRIVERS ARE ALWAYS CURSING OUR PEOPLE, MAKING THEM GIVE UP THEIR SEATS FOR WHITES.

AND IF THEY COMPLAIN THEY GET ARRESTED, RIGHT?

YES! BUT SO FAR NO CASE HAS EVER GONE TO THE FEDERAL COURT.

THIS HAS DENIED US THE CHANCE TO PUT THE BUS COMPANY AND THE CITY ON THE STAND FOR THEIR ILLEGAL PRACTICES.

DECEMBER 2, 1955.

YOU MAKE IT EASY ON YOURSELVES AND GIVE UP YOUR SEATS NOW.

YOU THERE! ARE YOU GOING TO GET UP OR WHAT?

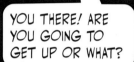

NO, I'M NOT.

HER NAME IS ROSA PARKS, AND, GET THIS, THE BUS DRIVER **DEMANDED** HER ARREST!

WELL, IT LOOKS LIKE WE'VE GOT OUR CASE!

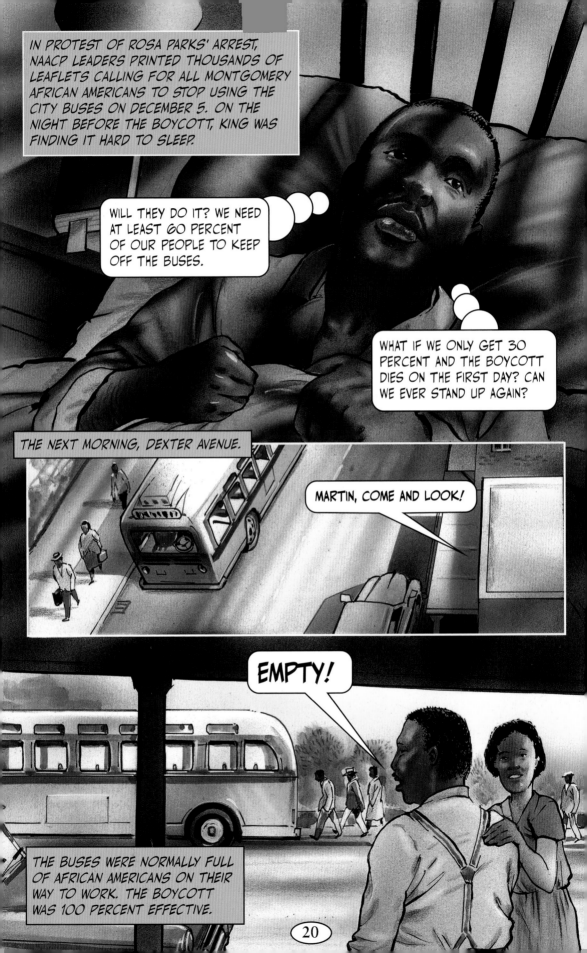

BY THAT EVENING, THE LOCAL LEADERS HAD FORMED THE MONTGOMERY IMPROVEMENT ASSOCIATION (MIA) AND ELECTED MARTIN LUTHER KING JR. AS THEIR LEADER. AT HOLT STREET BAPTIST CHURCH, HE SPOKE AT THE FIRST MASS MEETING.

WE ALL KNOW WHAT HAPPENED TO ROSA PARKS AND OF ALL THE INDIGNITIES WE BLACKS HAVE SUFFERED ON THE BUSES.

IF WE PROTEST COURAGEOUSLY, AND YET WITH DIGNITY AND LOVE, WHEN THE HISTORY BOOKS ARE WRITTEN, THEN SOMEBODY WILL HAVE TO SAY...

...THERE LIVED A RACE OF PEOPLE WHO HAD THE MORAL COURAGE TO STAND UP FOR THEIR RIGHTS, AND FOR WHAT THEY BELIEVED!

HIS SPEECH ELECTRIFIED THE CONGREGATION. A LIST OF DEMANDS, TO BE SENT TO THE AUTHORITIES, WAS APPROVED BY THE CROWD. THE FIGHT WAS ON.

FZZZT!

KAABOOOOM!

LUCKILY, NO ONE WAS HURT.

LATER, AN ANGRY CROWD GATHERED.

MY WIFE AND BABY ARE ALL RIGHT. PLEASE DO NOT RETALIATE. REMEMBER, LET NO MAN LAY YOU SO LOW AS TO MAKE YOU HATE HIM.

LATER, THE CITY DECLARED THE BUS BOYCOTT ILLEGAL. KING WAS AMONG EIGHTY-NINE AFRICAN AMERICANS ARRESTED FOR THEIR PART IN THE PROTEST. BUT THE MIA KEPT THE BOYCOTT GOING, FIRST WITH CHEAP TAXIS, AND THEN WITH A CARPOOL. THE CITY ASKED THE COURT TO SHUT DOWN THE CARPOOL.

IN NOVEMBER, IT LOOKED AS THOUGH THE CITY WAS GOING TO WIN, UNTIL...

THE SUPREME COURT RULES THAT ALABAMA'S SEGREGATION LAWS ARE...UNCONSTITUTIONAL!

HALLELUJAH, BROTHER!

BEFORE LONG...

LOOK AT THAT. COLORED AND WHITE FOLKS ARE SIDE BY SIDE!

YES, RALPH, A SMALL VICTORY...A BEGINNING!

23

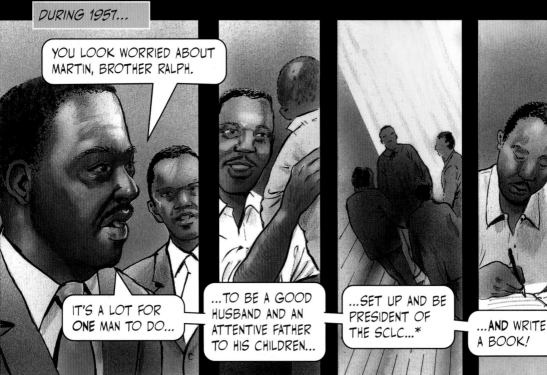

DURING 1957...

YOU LOOK WORRIED ABOUT MARTIN, BROTHER RALPH.

IT'S A LOT FOR ONE MAN TO DO...

...TO BE A GOOD HUSBAND AND AN ATTENTIVE FATHER TO HIS CHILDREN...

...SET UP AND BE PRESIDENT OF THE SCLC...*

...AND WRITE A BOOK!

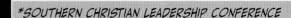

*SOUTHERN CHRISTIAN LEADERSHIP CONFERENCE

"STRIDE TOWARD FREEDOM: THE MONTGOMERY STORY" WAS PUBLISHED IN THE FALL. ON SEPTEMBER 20, KING WAS AT A BOOK SIGNING IN NEW YORK, WHEN...

MARTIN LUTHER KING, I'VE BEEN AFTER YOU FOR FIVE YEARS.

WHAT?

DR. KING HAS BEEN STABBED!

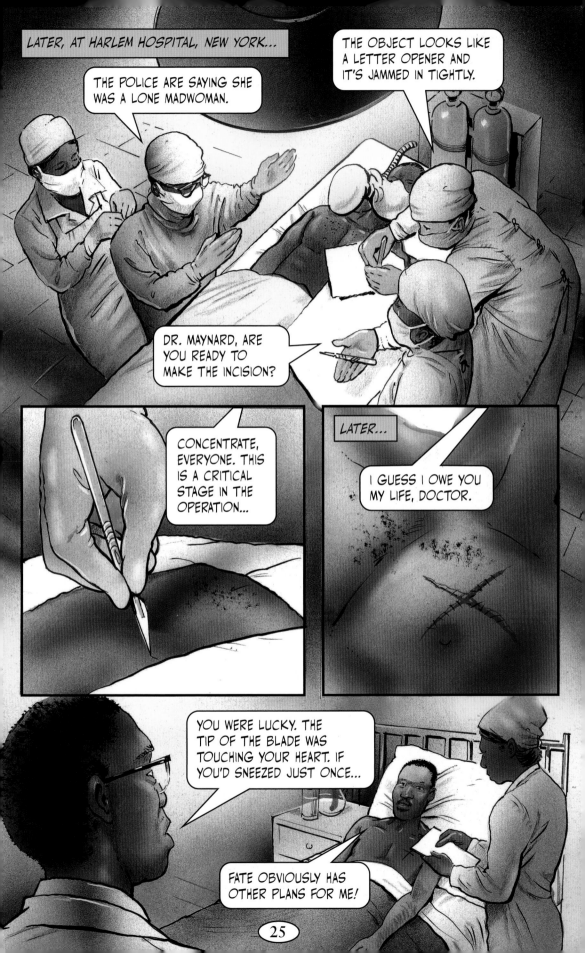

IN 1963, AFTER THE U.S. GOVERNMENT BROUGHT AN END TO INTERSTATE BUS SEGREGATION, THE SCLC WENT TO BIRMINGHAM, ALABAMA. HUNDREDS OF MARCHERS, INCLUDING KING, WERE IMPRISONED BY POLICE CHIEF BULL CONNOR. FROM HIS PRISON CELL, KING WROTE "A LETTER FROM BIRMINGHAM JAIL," WHICH WAS PUBLISHED ALL OVER THE WORLD.

LATE APRIL, SCLC HEADQUARTERS, BIRMINGHAM.

MARTIN, WHERE ARE WE GOING TO GET OUR MARCHERS FROM? EVERYONE'S IN JAIL!

HMMM...

MAY 3, 1963. IN BIRMINGHAM 2,500 CHILDREN JOINED KING AND OTHERS ON A MARCH INTO THE CITY.

DON'T GET TIRED. DON'T GET BITTER. ARE YOU TIRED?

NO!

BLOCKING THEIR WAY WAS CHIEF BULL CONNOR.

THE TIDE HAD TURNED. ON MAY 10, A GROUP OF LEADING BIRMINGHAM BUSINESSMEN AGREED TO END THEIR SEGREGATIONIST PRACTICES THROUGHOUT THE CITY.

THE CITY OF BIRMINGHAM HAS REACHED AN ACCORD WITH ITS CONSCIENCE. IT IS AN EXAMPLE OF PROGRESSIVE RACE RELATIONS.

ON JUNE 11, 1963, PRESIDENT KENNEDY ADDRESSED THE NATION.

I'M GOING TO ASK THE CONGRESS TO MAKE A COMMITMENT TO THE PROPOSITION THAT RACE HAS NO PLACE IN AMERICAN LIFE.

THE BILL WOULD EFFECTIVELY OUTLAW SEGREGATION IN PUBLIC FACILITIES ACROSS AMERICA.

ON JUNE 22, KING MET WITH THE PRESIDENT.

NOW IS **NOT** THE RIGHT TIME FOR A MARCH ON WASHINGTON, DR. KING.

WE WANT THE CIVIL RIGHTS BILL TO SUCCEED IN CONGRESS. A MASS DEMONSTRATION WOULD BE ILL-TIMED.

FRANKLY, I HAVE NEVER TAKEN PART IN ANY DIRECT-ACTION MOVEMENT THAT DID **NOT** SEEM ILL-TIMED. MANY PEOPLE THOUGHT THAT **BIRMINGHAM** WAS ILL-TIMED.

I TAKE YOUR POINT, BUT TO LOSE THE FIGHT IN CONGRESS WOULD BE A TERRIBLE THING. IT COULD BRING THE WHOLE ADMINISTRATION **DOWN**. WE'RE UP TO OUR NECKS IN THIS THING!

MR. PRESIDENT, THE AMERICAN AMERICANS' PATIENCE IS AT AN END. A MASS MARCH WOULD BE A WAY FOR MY PEOPLE TO CHANNEL THEIR ANGER—A CALM, **CONSTRUCTIVE** WAY FOR THEM TO EXPRESS THEIR GRIEVANCES.

ON AUGUST 28, 1963, THE MARCH ON WASHINGTON FOR AFRICAN AMERICAN JOBS AND FREEDOM TOOK PLACE. IT WAS ATTENDED BY MORE THAN 250,000 PEOPLE AT THE LINCOLN MEMORIAL. ALONG WITH MANY OTHERS, KING DELIVERED A ROUSING EIGHT-MINUTE SPEECH. TOWARD THE END, HE LOOKED AWAY FROM HIS NOTES TO SAY...

I HAVE A DREAM TODAY.

I HAVE A DREAM THAT ONE DAY, DOWN IN ALABAMA WITH ITS FIERCE RACISTS...THAT ONE DAY, RIGHT THERE IN ALABAMA...

...LITTLE BLACK BOYS AND BLACK GIRLS WILL BE ABLE TO JOIN HANDS WITH LITTLE WHITE BOYS AND WHITE GIRLS AS SISTERS AND BROTHERS.

I HAVE A *DREAM* TODAY.

...WHEN ALL GOD'S CHILDREN, BLACK MEN AND WHITE MEN, JEWS AND GENTILES, PROTESTANTS AND CATHOLICS, WILL BE ABLE TO JOIN HANDS AND SING...

...FREE AT LAST! FREE AT LAST! THANK GOD ALMIGHTY, WE ARE FREE AT LAST!

AS THEY WALKED DEEPER INTO THE COUNTRY...

SEE THAT CHURCH, WITH ITS ROOF HALF OFF?

THAT IS WHY WE'RE MARCHING!

PEOPLE, MARTIN IS OUR BLACK MOSES SENT BY GOD TO LEAD US FROM THE WILDERNESS!

THAT'S **THE** MARTIN LUTHER KING! I HAVE KISSED **THE** MARTIN LUTHER KING!

ON MARCH 25, KING LED 25,000 MARCHERS INTO MONTGOMERY. ON AUGUST 6, 1965, PRESIDENT JOHNSON SIGNED A BILL INTO LAW THAT ALLOWED AFRICAN AMERICANS TO REGISTER TO VOTE.

IN 1967, KING BEGAN PLANNING A MASS DEMONSTRATION THAT WOULD TAKE PLACE IN WASHINGTON. THE ISSUE WOULD BE POVERTY AND THE PROTEST WOULD LAST THREE MONTHS AND INVOLVE HUNDREDS OF THOUSANDS OF PEOPLE.

THE LEADERS OF A BLACK YOUTH GROUP IN MEMPHIS, TENNESSEE, WERE NOT IMPRESSED WHEN THEY READ OF KING'S PLAN.

NONVIOLENCE? DO THEY REALLY THINK THAT'S GOING TO CHANGE THE MINDS OF THE PEOPLE RUNNING THIS COUNTRY?

WE WILL BRING THE CAPITOL TO A STANDSTILL AND **MAKE** THIS GOVERNMENT LISTEN AND RESPOND TO THE NEEDS OF THE POOR.

THE GREAT MARCH WAS PLANNED FOR SPRING 1968. BUT SOME AFRICAN AMERICANS WERE GROWING RESTLESS WITH THE SLOW PACE OF CHANGE.

KING ISN'T GOING TO **GET** US ANYTHING. IF WE WANT OUR RIGHTS, WE'VE GOT TO **TAKE** THEM!

ON MARCH 28, 1968, KING WAS IN MEMPHIS ATTENDING A MARCH WHEN...

CRASH!

THE MEMPHIS POLICE WERE QUICK TO RESPOND. KING WAS DISTRAUGHT.

FZZZZZT!

WE HAVE TO GET YOU OUT OF HERE, DR. KING!

PLEASE, I MUST CALL IT OFF! I WILL NOT LEAD A VIOLENT MARCH!

BLUE STALLION Lounge

THE RIOT MADE THE NATIONAL PRESS.

"DR. KING'S POSE AS THE LEADER OF A PEACEFUL MOVEMENT HAS BEEN SHATTERED." BOY, THEY'RE REALLY DOING A NUMBER ON YOU, MARTIN.

I HAVE TO COME BACK AND PROVE THEM WRONG!

EVEN THOUGH THERE'S A PRICE ON YOUR HEAD?*

*ABERNATHY HAD HEARD A RUMOR OF AN OFFER OF $50,000 FOR KING'S ASSASSINATION.

THE LORRAINE MOTEL, MEMPHIS, APRIL 4. KING RETURNED TO LEAD ANOTHER MARCH FOR THE CITY WORKERS.

MARTIN, I'LL BE RIGHT OUT!

OK, RALPH. I'LL JUST WAIT HERE.

BANG!

MARTIN, THIS IS ME, RALPH. DON'T BE AFRAID...DON'T...

OH, NO! MARTIN'S BEEN SHOT!

THE END

THE PROMISED LAND

Martin Luther King Jr. died on the operating table at St. Joseph's Hospital in Memphis, at 7:05 PM on April 4, 1968. Following the official announcement, feelings of grief, guilt, and rage gripped America.

SHOCK WAVES

Riots in response to King's assassination erupted in 110 cities, including Washington, D.C. Seventy-five thousand troops and national guardsmen had to be sent out to restore order. As tributes poured in from around the world, a massive manhunt was under way for the assassin.

James Earl Ray, an escaped convict, was finally arrested, tried, and found guilty of King's murder. He was later sentenced to 99 years in prison without parole.

KING HONORED

After an emotional service attended by

MASS MOURNING

More than 60,000 people traveled to Atlanta, Georgia, on April 9, 1968, to attend Martin Luther King Jr.'s funeral. His coffin was carried through the city on a cart drawn by two mules to represent his planned campaign for the poor.

mourners of many races at Ebenezer Baptist Church in Atlanta, King's coffin was brought to Morehouse College. Here, a eulogy was delivered by his old tutor, Dr. Benjamin Mays. "Martin Luther faced the dogs, the police, jail, heavy criticism, and finally death; and he never carried a gun, not even a knife to defend himself. He had only his faith to rely on."

KING'S LEGACY

When Martin Luther King Jr. died, America lost a great leader. Even now, he still serves as a role model for society.

It is hard for young people growing up in America today to fully imagine living in the segregated society of the 1960s. This is due, in a large part, to Martin Luther King Jr.'s efforts toward social equality.

King also worked tirelessly to ensure that African Americans would have the right to vote. This has led to African Americans becoming mayors, judges, and prominent politicians. Modern-day figures such as Colin Powell and Condoleezza Rice have risen high in society thanks, in part, to Martin Luther King Jr.

FORCE OF LAW
President Lyndon B. Johnson signed into law the Civil Rights Act of 1965, a direct result of King's influence.

SELECTED WRITINGS AND SPEECHES OF MARTIN LUTHER KING JR.

The purity of his message, and the eloquent way he delivered it, give Martin Luther King Jr.'s words a powerful relevance today.

SPEECHES

MIA Mass Meeting at Holt Street Baptist Church (1955)
"Give Us the Ballot" (1957)
"I Have a Dream" (1963)
"I've Been to the Mountaintop" (1968)
"Beyond Vietnam" (1968)

WRITINGS

Stride Toward Freedom: The Montgomery Story (1958)
Strength to Love (1963)
"Letter from Birmingham Jail" (1963)
Why We Can't Wait (1964)
The Trumpet of Conscience (1968)
Where Do We Go From Here: Chaos or Community? (1968)

GLOSSARY

accord An agreement.

assassination Killing a person, often secretly, and always planned in advance. Assassinations are often carried out for political reasons.

civil war A war where divisions within a group fight each other. The American Civil War lasted from 1861 to 1865.

congregation A group of people at a church.

constitution An accepted law or custom, or set of laws and customs.

enroll To sign up.

equality When everyone is treated the same.

graduate A person who has passed all examinations in a university.

hostile Unfriendly toward someone.

humiliation Making fun of a person to cause embarrassment while destroying his or her self-respect and dignity.

illegal An action that breaks the law.

indignity An action that makes a person feel worthless.

Ku Klux Klan A organization of white people who believe in white supremacy and who harass, and sometimes murder, nonwhite citizens.

moral An issue of right or wrong.

mourner An individual who is deeply upset following the death of another person.

nonviolence When peace is used instead of war.

perpetrate To carry out or bring about an action or event that is either illegal or linked to a crime.

preacher Someone who gives a sermon as part of a religious service.

protest A solemn announcement or disagreement, either with a person or a law. A protest can be violent or nonviolent.

racist Someone who believes that a person's race affects their character, and that differences between races lead to the people of some races being superior to others.

riot To harm people and destroy property out of anger.

segregation The splitting off of a certain group away from the rest of society.

sniper Someone who kills or injures others by shooting them with a gun, usually from a concealed place.

supremacist Someone who believes that he or she is better than others because of his or her race.

theology The study of religious beliefs.

unconstitutional When an action goes against accepted laws or customs.

under the wing To be guided or protected by another person who is typically older and has more experience.

veteran Somebody who has been doing something for a very long time.

FOR MORE INFORMATION

ORGANIZATIONS

The King Center
449 Auburn Avenue, N.E.
Atlanta, GA 30312
(404) 526-8900
E-mail: information@thekingcenter.org
Web site: http://www.thekingcenter.org/

National Civil Rights Museum
450 Mulberry Street
Memphis, TN 38103
(901) 521-9699
Web site: http://www.civilrightsmuseum.org

FOR FURTHER READING

King Jr., Martin Luther, and Clayborne Carson (ed.). *The Autobiography of Martin Luther King Jr.* South Victoria, Australia: Warner Books, 2001.

King Jr., Martin Luther, Coretta Scott King, and Dexter Scott King. *The Martin Luther King, Jr. Companion: Quotations from the Speeches, Essays, and Books of Martin Luther King Jr.* New York, NY: St. Martin's Press, 1998.

Levine, Ellen, and Beth Peck (illustrator). *If You Lived at the Time of Martin Luther King.* New York, NY: Scholastic Paperbacks, 1994.

Marzollo, J. and Brian Pin Kney (illustrator). *Happy Birthday, Martin Luther King.* New York, NY: Scholastic Press, 1993.

Millender, Dharathula H. *Martin Luther King Jr.: Young Man with a Dream.* New York, NY: Aladdin, 1986.

INDEX

Web Sites

Due to the changing nature of Internet links, the Rosen Publishing Group, Inc., has developed an online list of Web sites related to the subject of this book. This site is updated regularly. Please use this link to access the list:

http://www.rosenlinks.com/grbi/mlkj